MY DISNEY

STARS AND FRIENDS 3

Workbook and eBook

Kathryn Harper

Contents

1 My animals

1

2

1 Match and say.

2 1.4 What can you hear? Draw and say.

1

2

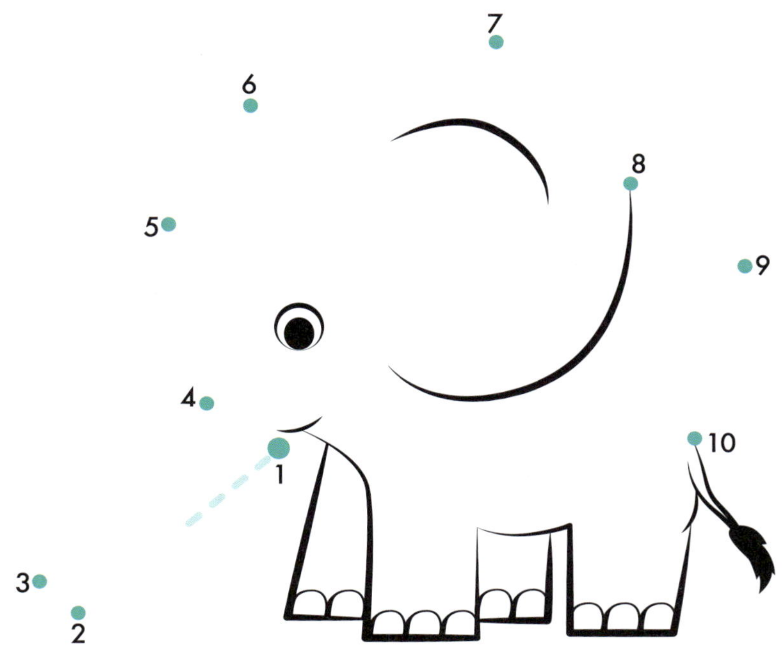

1 1.8 **Listen, match, and say.**

2 **What's this? Join the dots and say.**

I'm curious

1

2

1 What can you see? Color and say.

2 What makes you curious? Think and check (✔).

1

2

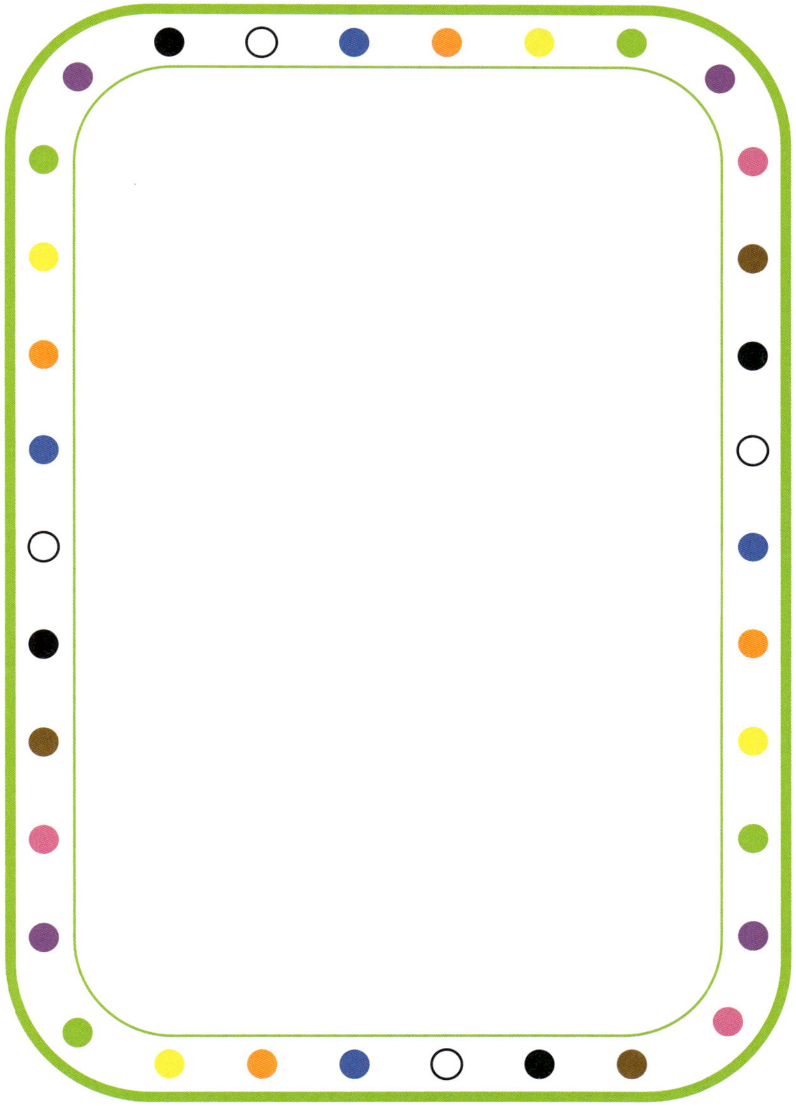

1 Look and color.

2 What's your favorite animal? Draw, color, and say.

What's this?

❶ 🎧 1.16 **Order the story (1–6). Then listen and check.**

❷ **What is Simba curious about? Circle.**

1

2

1 1.18 **Listen, circle, and say.**

2 **Which new things do you try? Draw and say.**

Animals and me

1 1.20 **Listen and point.** 2 **Match and say.**
3 **What's missing? Draw and match.**

1

2

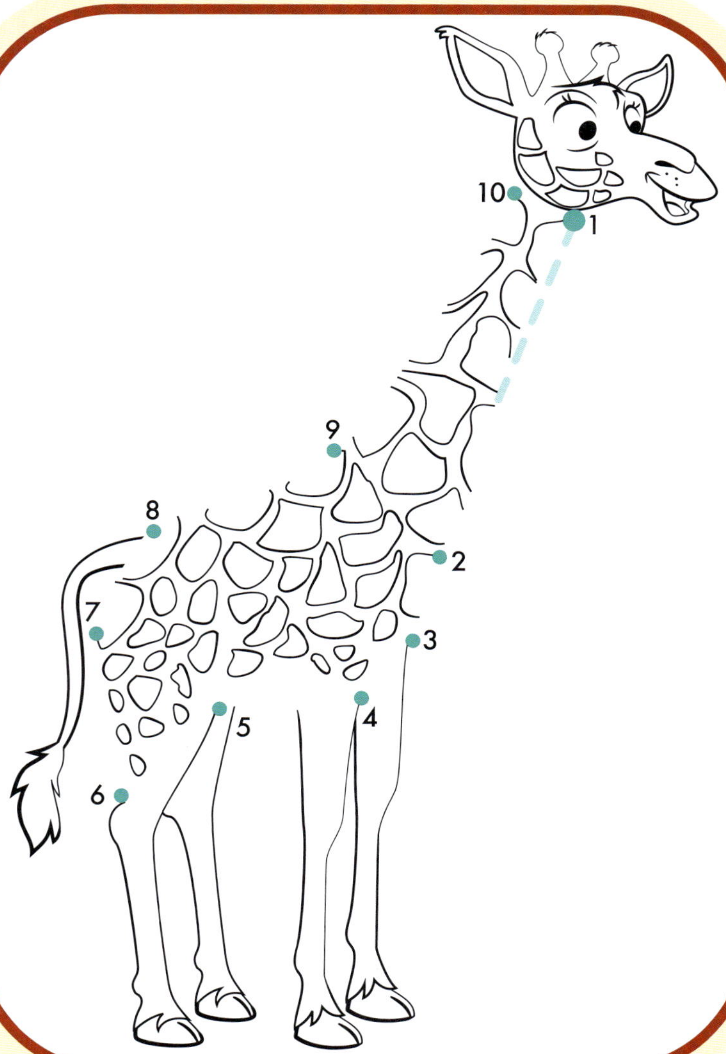

1 1.22 **Listen and circle.**
2 **What's this? Join the dots and say.** 3 **Color your star.**

2 My party

1

2

1 2.4 Listen, trace, and say.

2 What's missing? Draw and say.

1

2

1 2.9 **Listen, match, and say.**
2 **What would you like? Draw and say.**

Lesson 3 ○ Feelings

I'm surprised

1

2

1 **Who is surprised? Circle and say.**

2 **What makes you surprised? Think and check (✓).**

1 2 ___ 4 ___ 6 ___ 8 ___ 10

1 2.14 Listen, draw, and say.

2 Trace, write, and say.

Peter Pan's party

1 2.16 **Order the story (1–6). Then listen and check.**

2 **Who is your favorite character? Circle and say.**

1

2

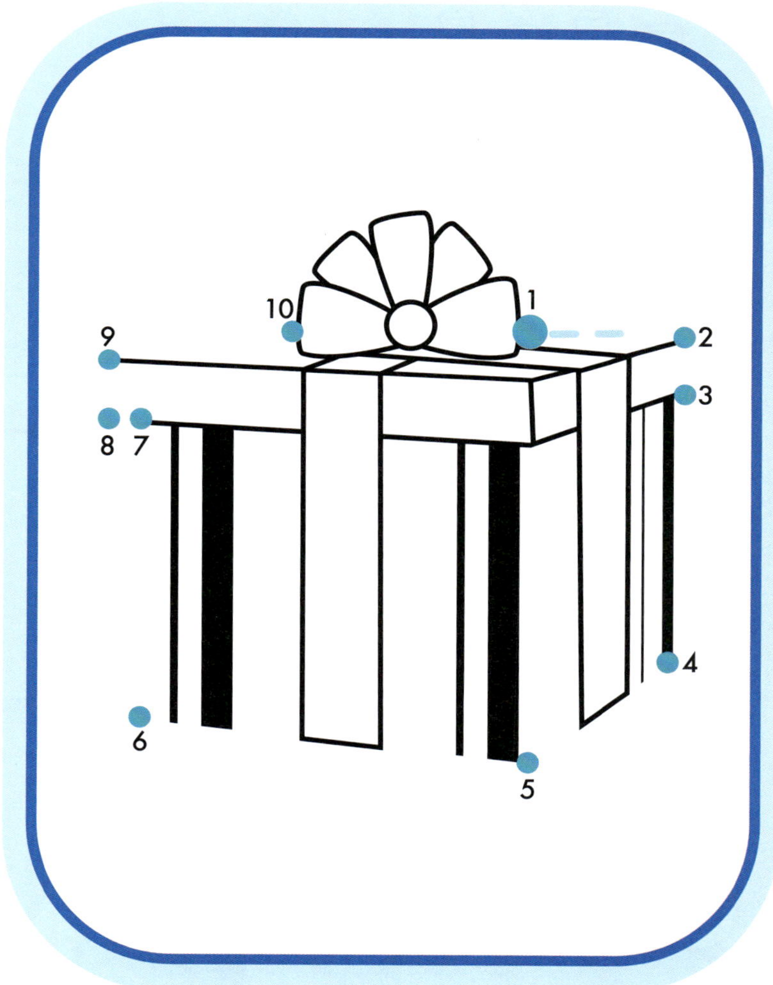

❶ **Who is polite? Check (✓) or cross (✕).**
❷ **Join the dots and say.**

Lesson 6 ○ Real world

My party

1

2

3

4

5

1 2.20 **Listen and point.** **2** **Match and say.**
3 **What would you like? Color and say.**

1

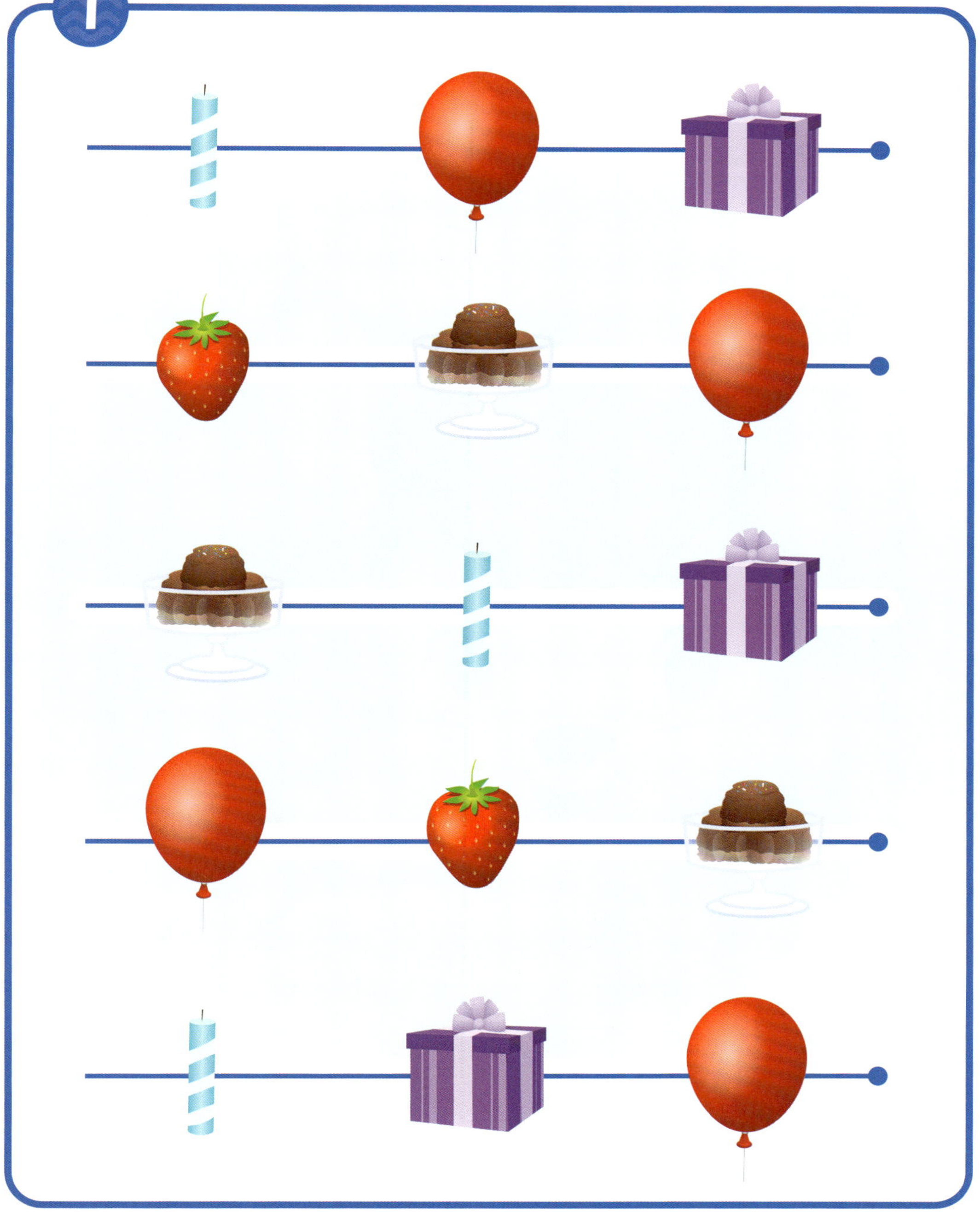

2

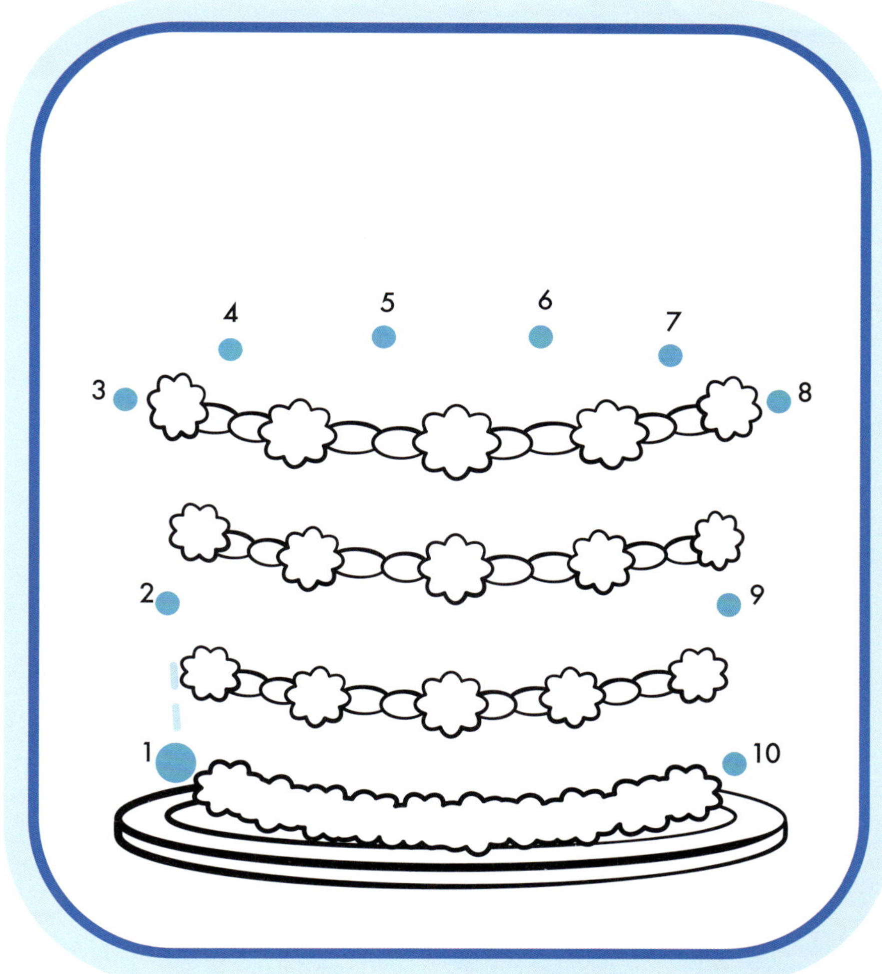

1 2.22 Listen and circle.
2 What's this? Join the dots and say. 3 Color your star.

3 In the woods

1 3.3 Listen, point, and say.
2 Color and say.

The bee is on the ...

1

2

3

1 3.7 **Listen, say, and match.**

2 **Draw a bee on the flower.** 3 **Draw a bee in the flower.**

Lesson 3 ○ Feelings

I love ...

1 3.10 **Listen and point.** 2 **Trace and say.**

3 **What do you love? Draw and say.**

A lot of shapes

1

2

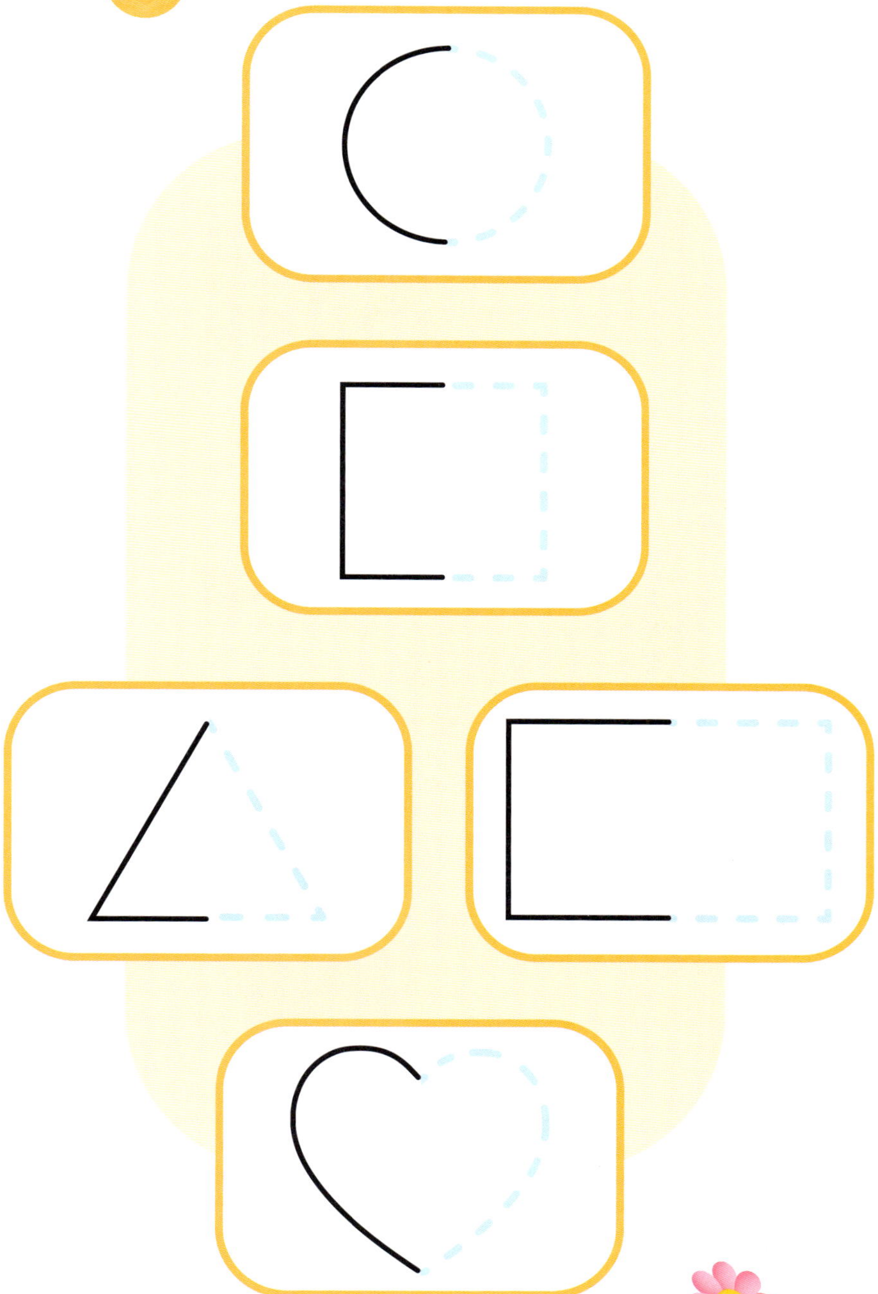

1 Match and say.

2 Trace and say.

Where's the ant?

1 3.13 **What do they love? Listen, circle, and say.**

2 **Who is your favorite character? Check (✓) and say.**

1

2

1 Who cares about nature? Check (✓) and say.

2 What do you care about? Draw and say.

Amazing nature

1

2

1 Match and say.

2 What's your favorite tree? Draw and say.

1

2

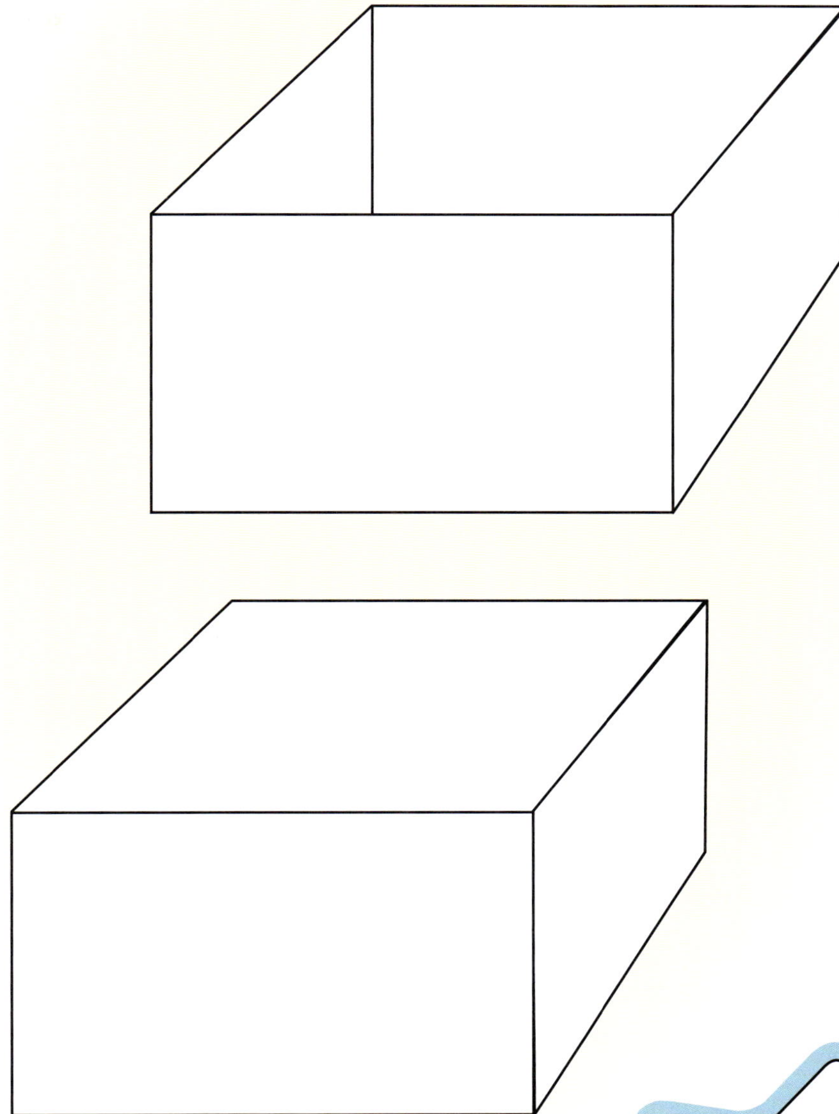

1 Match and say.

2 3.17 Listen, draw, and say. 3 Color your star.

4 In the sky

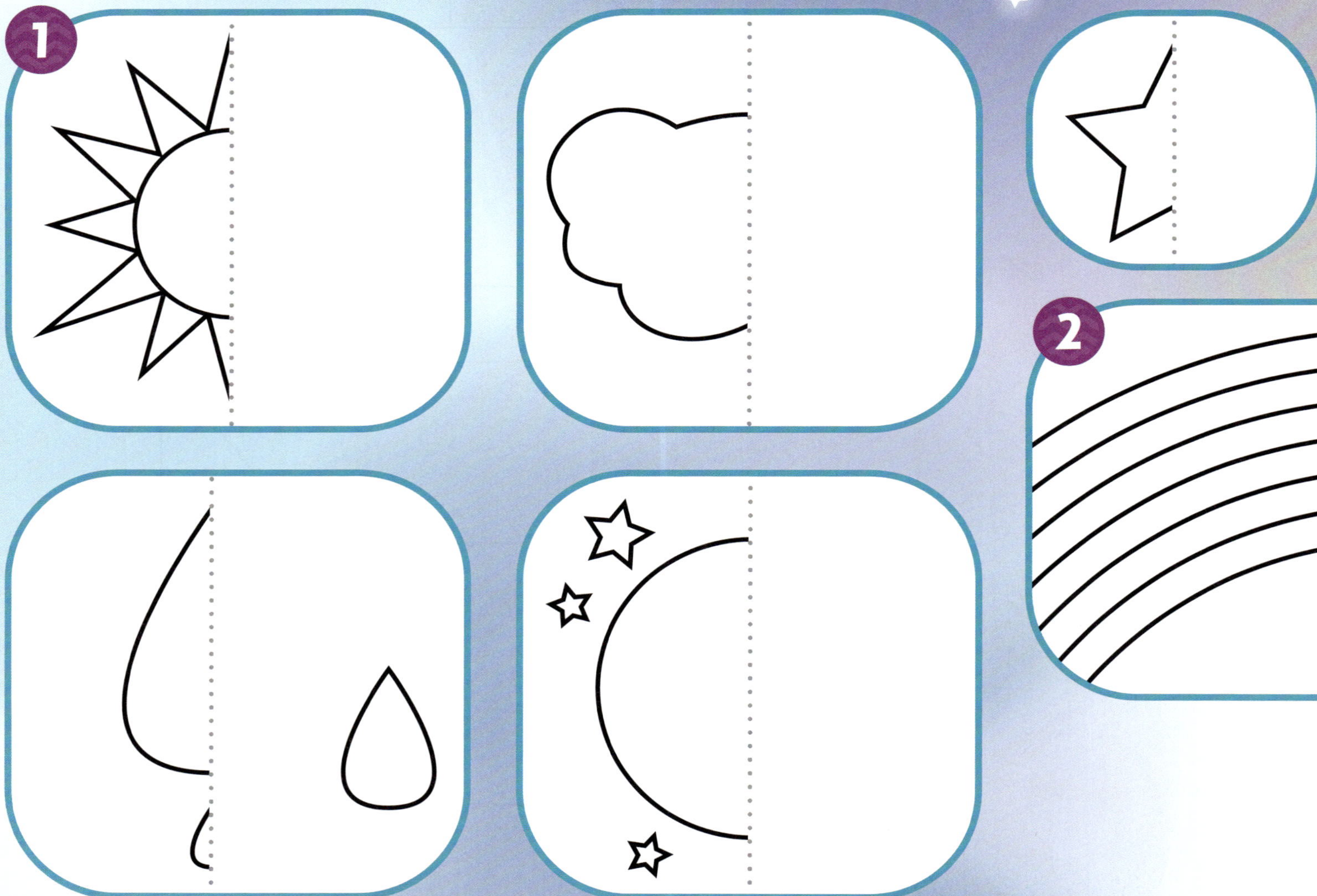

1

2

1 4.3 **Listen, draw, and say.**
2 **Draw and color the rainbow.**

1

2

1 4.7 Listen, number, and say.

2 What can you see in the sky today? Draw and say.

I feel safe

1

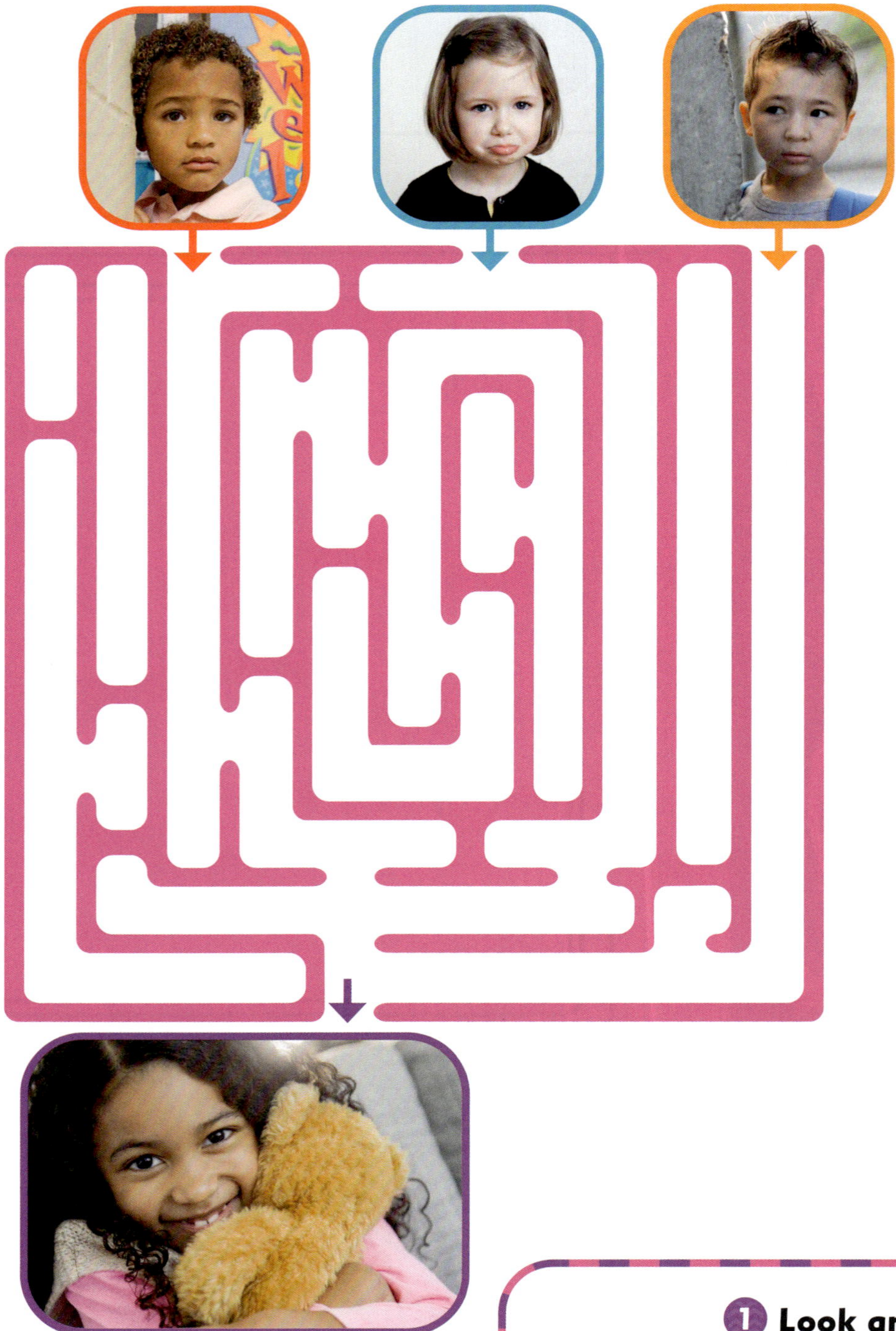

2

1 Look and draw lines.

2 What makes you feel safe? Draw and say.

A lot of shapes

1 4.13 Listen, find, and color.

2 How many? Count and write.

Lesson 5A ○ Storytime

Where's my rainbow?

1 (audio) 4.15 **Trace. Then listen and point.**

2 **Color and say.**

1 4.17 **Listen, number, and say.**

2 **How do you help?**

Day or night?

1

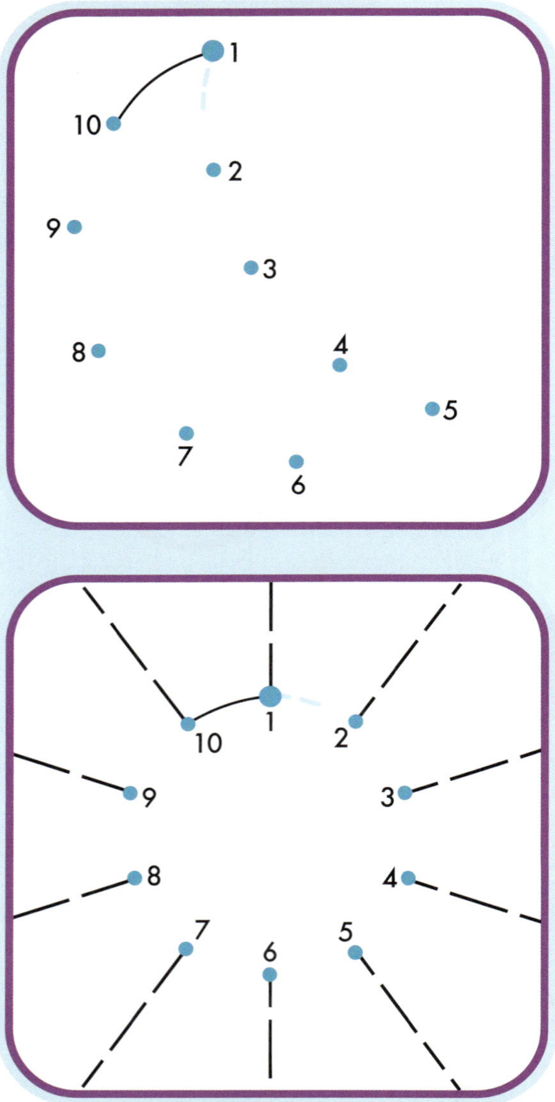

2

1 What are they? Join the dots and say.
2 Match and say.

1

2

1 What's in the big picture? Circle and say.
2 How many? Count and write. 3 Color your star.

5 My senses

1

2

1 5.4 Listen, match, and say.

2 What can the mouse hear? Join the dots and say.

1

2

1 5.8 Listen, find, and circle.
2 What can you taste? Draw and say.

Lesson 3 ○ Feelings

I'm sad

1 

2 

3 

4 

1 5.11 Listen, match, and say.

2 What makes you sad? Check (✔).

1

(flower)	11	12	13	14	15
(flamingo)	11	12	13	14	15
(butterfly)	11	12	13	14	15
(rose)	11	12	13	14	15
(mushroom)	11	12	13	14	15

2

12	13	14	....
10	11	12	....
8	9	10	....
11	12	13	....
9	10	11	....

1 How many? Count, circle, and say.
2 What's next? Write and say.

Lesson 5A ○ Storytime

Where's the rabbit?

1 5.15 Order the story (1–6). Then listen and check.

2 What color is the Cheshire Cat? Color and say.

1

2

3

4

1 5.17 Listen and match.

2 What can you do? Draw a smile and say.

My house

1

2

3

4

1 5.19 Listen and draw.

2 Show and tell.

1

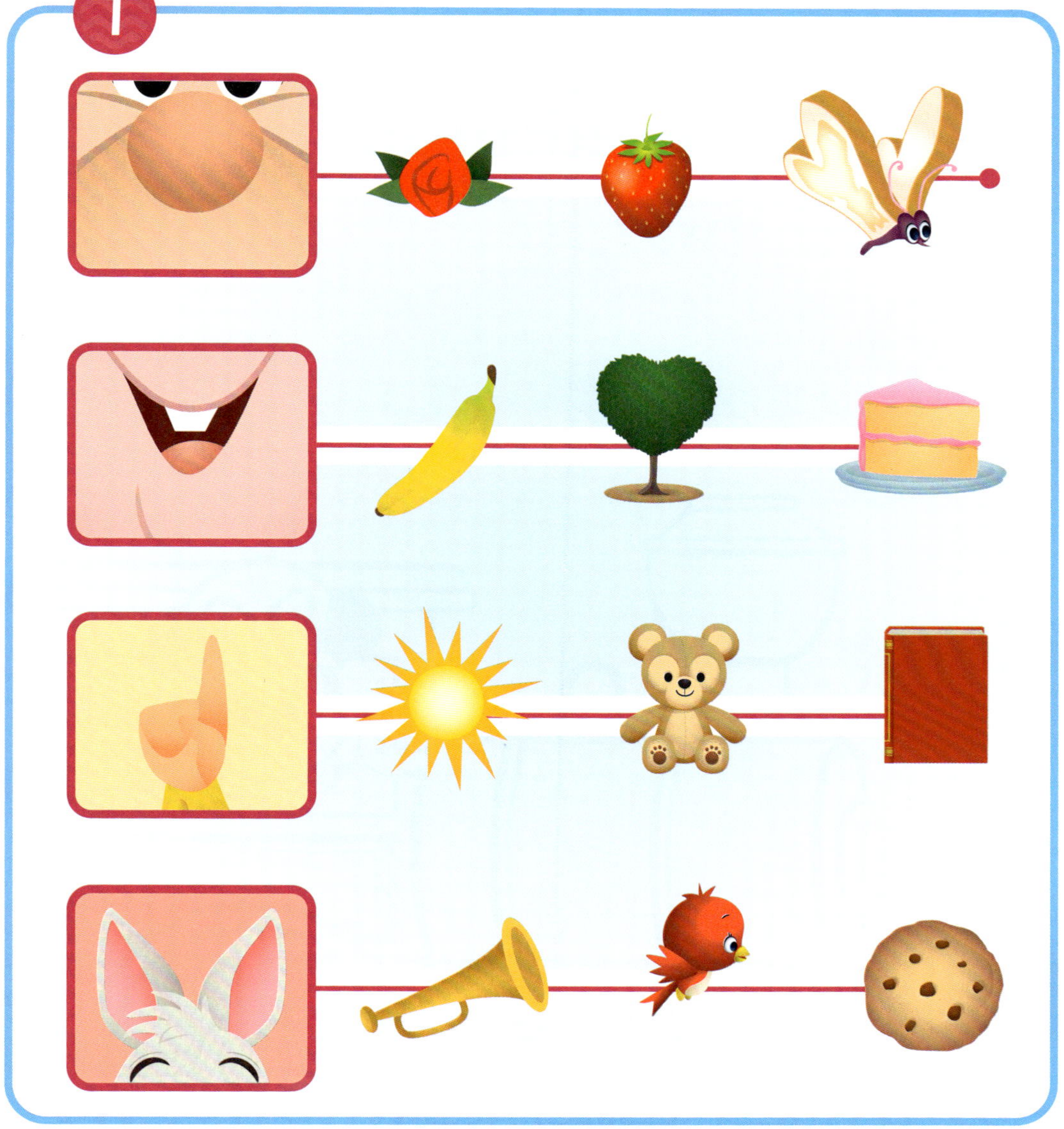

2

1 Circle the odd one out. Then say.
2 What can you see? Draw, color, and say. 3 Color your star.

6 Let's go!

1

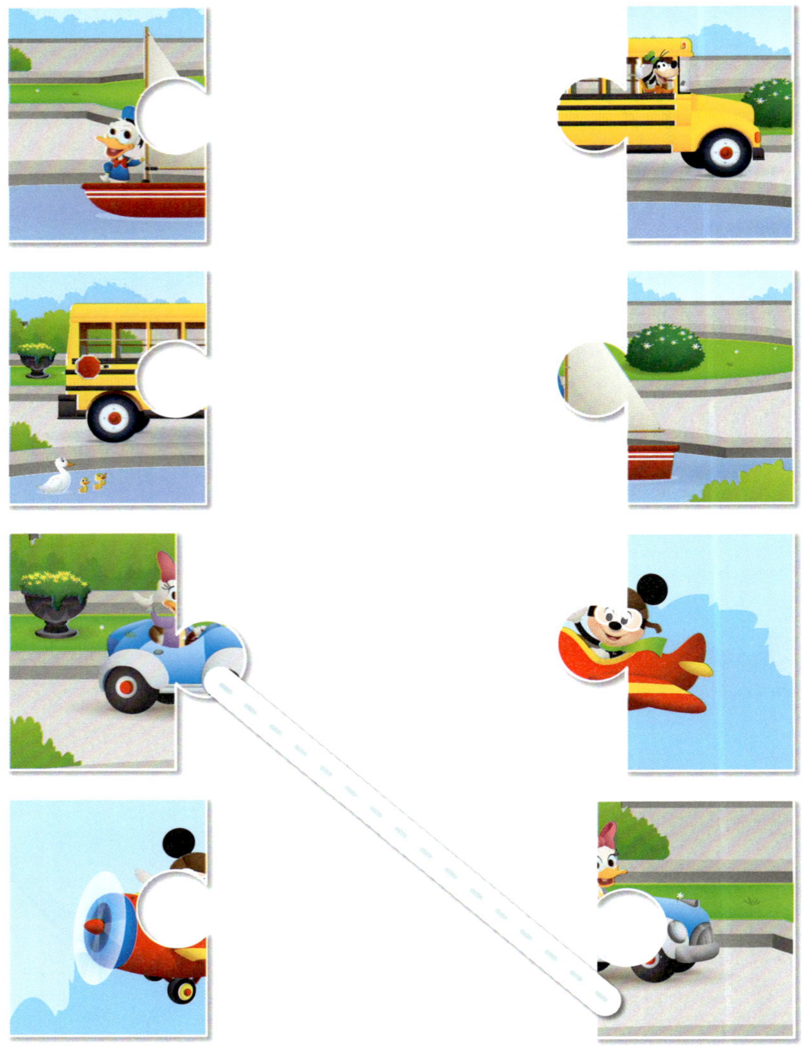

2

1 6.4 Listen, match, and say.
2 Color Minnie's train.

1

2

1 6.8 **Match. Then listen, point, and say.**

2 **Draw a bus from your city and say.**

Lesson 3 ◦ Feelings

I'm excited

1

2

1 6.12 **Who is excited? Trace, listen, and say.**

2 **What makes you excited? Look, check (✓), and say.**

1

3

1	2	3	4	5	6	7	8	9	10	11	12	13	14	15

1 4 7 10 13

2 5 8 11 14

3 6 9 12 15

1 Think and color. 2 6.14 Listen, check, and say.
3 Color, point, and say.

Lesson 5A ○ Storytime

Be careful!

1 6.16 **Order the story (1–6). Then listen and check.**

2 **Who helps Minnie? Circle.**

1

2

3

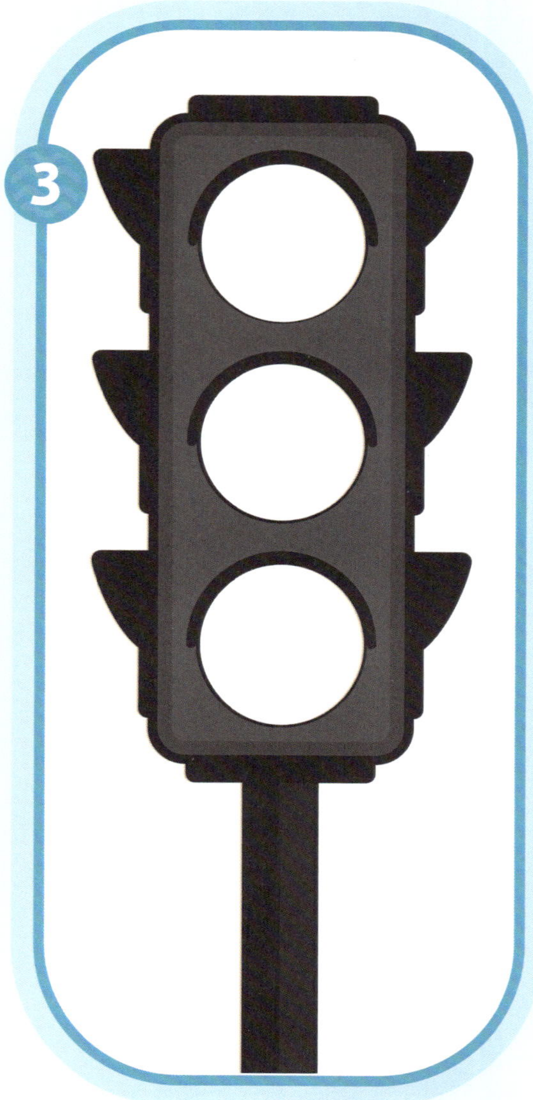

1 Why does Mickey say *Be careful?* Check (✓) and say.
2 Are the children careful? Match and say. 3 Color and say.

Toy transport

1

2

1 6.19 **Listen, match, and say.**

2 **What do you have? Draw and say.**

1

2

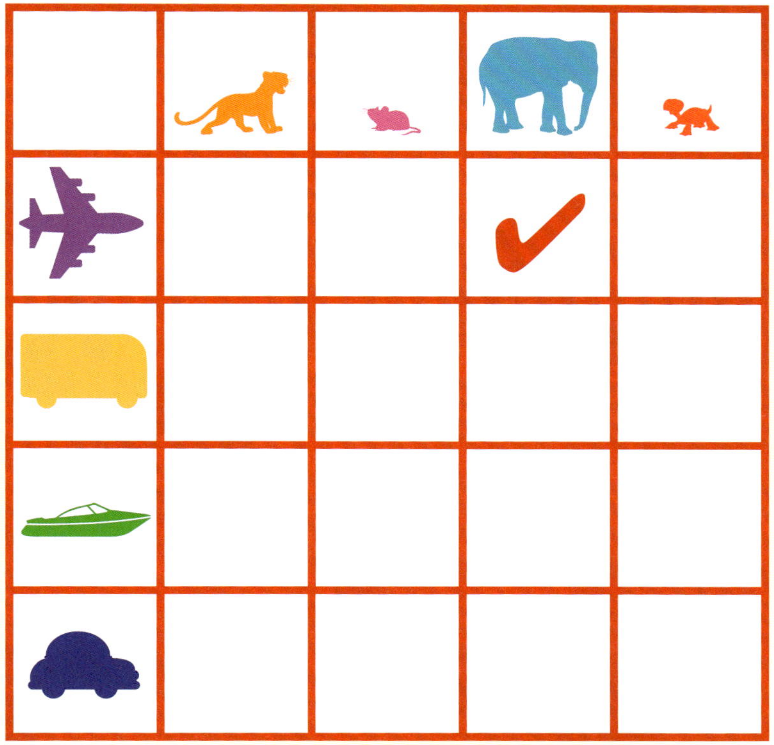

1 6.21 Listen and number.
2 6.22 Listen and check (✓). 3 Color your star.

7 In the ocean

1 7.3 Listen, match, and say.

2 Which is your favorite? Circle and say.

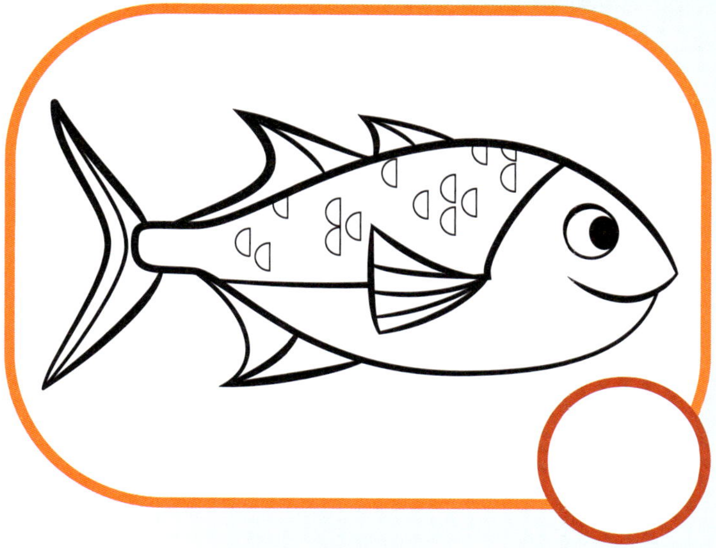

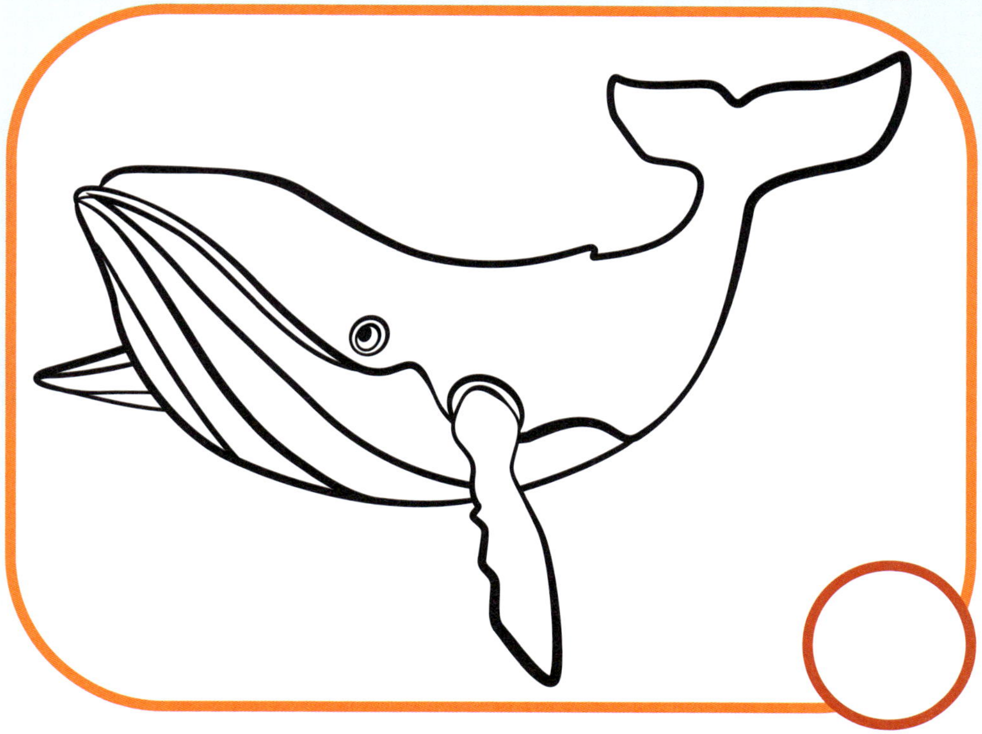

1 7.7 Listen and color. Say.

2 Which sea animals have two colors? Check (✓).

I'm scared

1

2

1 Who is scared? Trace and say.

2 What makes you feel scared? Draw and say.

1

15 16 17 18 19 20

15 16 17 18 19 20

15 16 17 18 19 20

2

1	2	....	4	5
6	....	8	9	10
11	12	13	....	15
16	17	18	19	....

1 How many? Count and circle.
2 Write the missing numbers.

What is it?

1 7.13 **Order the story (1–6). Then listen and check.**

2 **Who is your favorite character? Circle and say.**

1

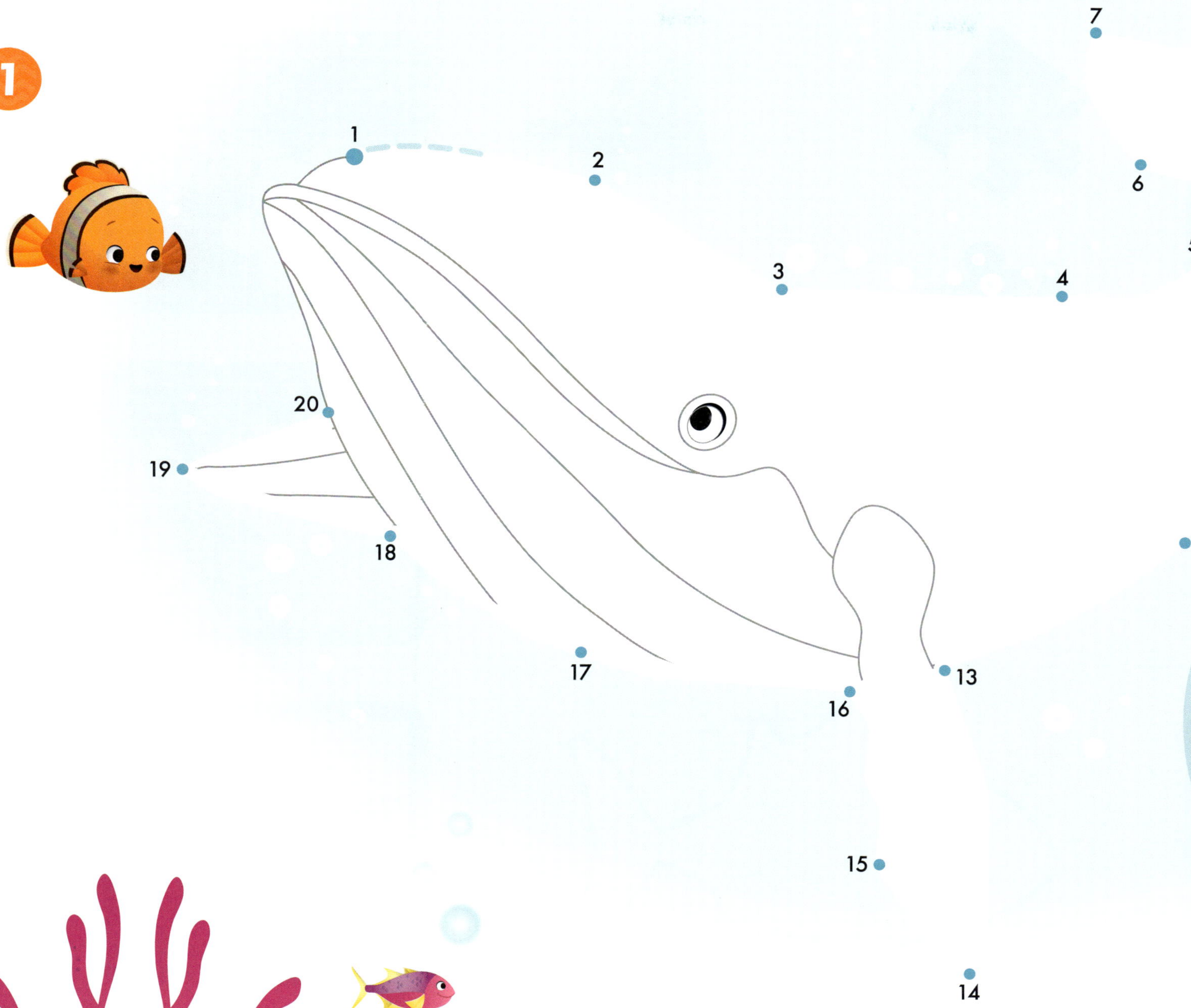

2

1 Why is Nemo brave? Join the dots and say.
2 When are you brave? Draw.

Ocean colors

1

2

1 Match and say.

2 What color is your favorite fish? Color and say.

1

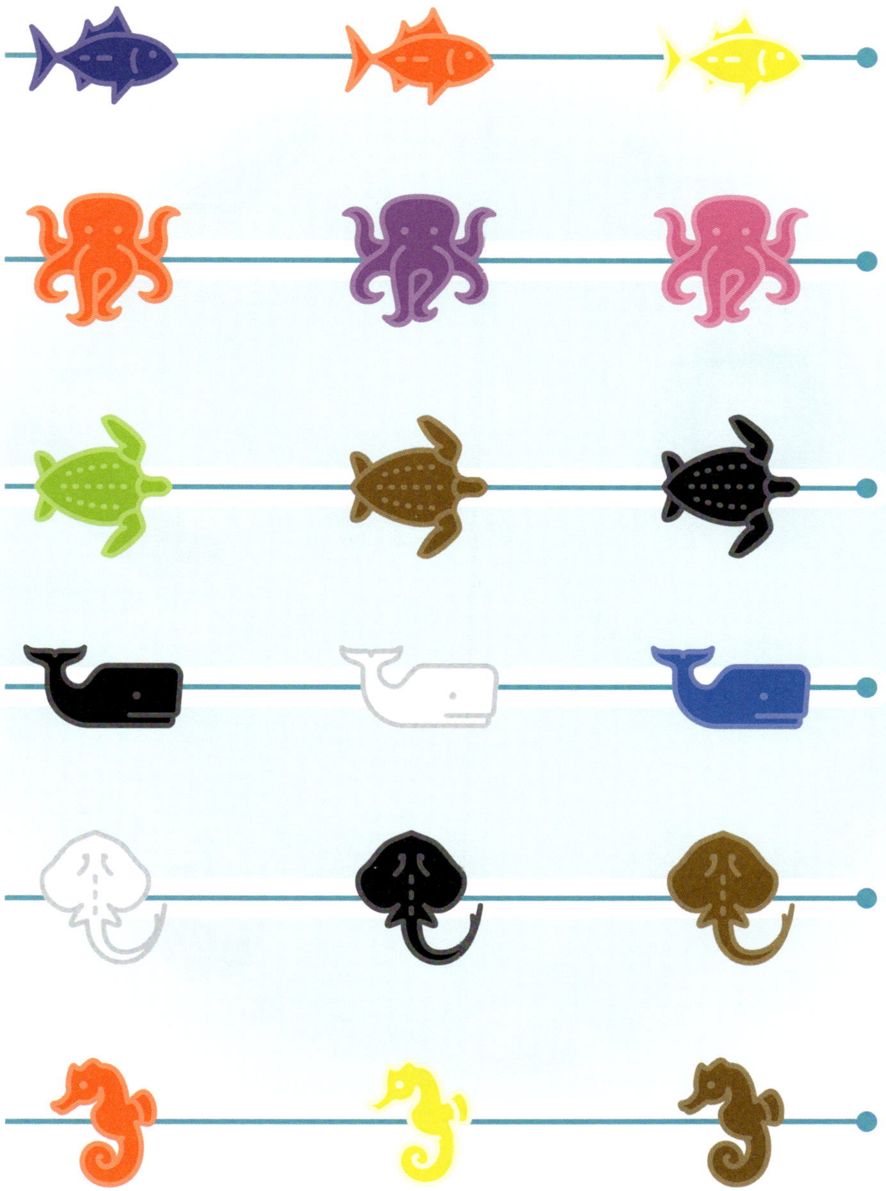

2

1 2 3 4

1 7.17 Listen and circle.
2 Color and say. 3 Color your star.

8 My city

Lesson 1 ○ Vocabulary

City places

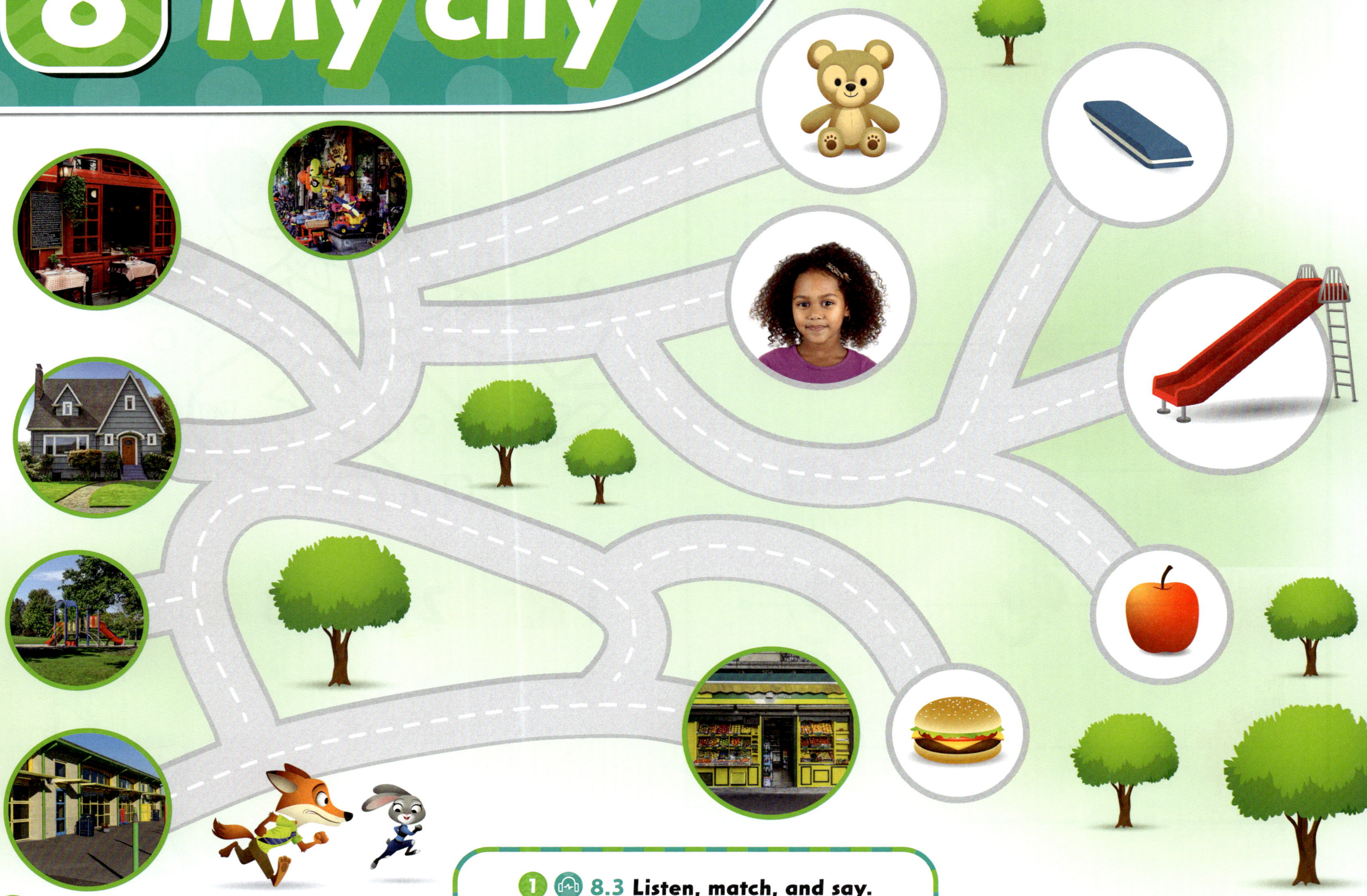

1 8.3 Listen, match, and say.

2 Where are you now? Circle and say.

1

2

1 Match and say.
2 Color and say.

I'm proud of ...

1

2

1 **Who is proud? Trace and say.**

2 **What are you proud of? Draw and say.**

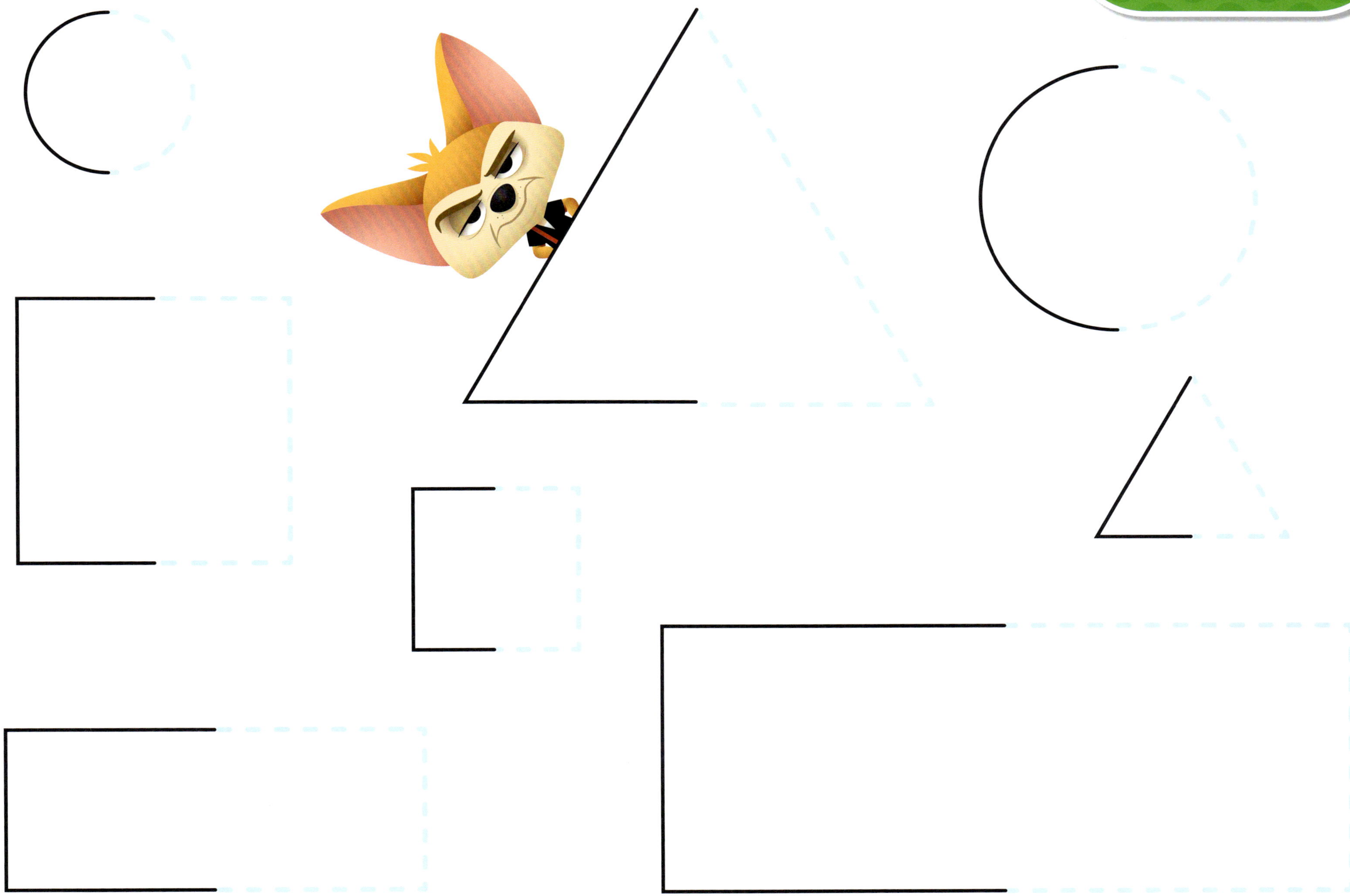

1 Trace and say.
2 8.11 Listen and color.

Where's Fru Fru?

1 8.13 **Order the story (1–6). Then listen and check.**

2 **Who feels proud? Circle.**

1

2

1 Who makes an effort? Color the star.

2 When do you make an effort? Draw and say.

Fun places

1

1

2

3

4

2

1 8.16 **Listen and draw lines to match.**

2 **Where would you like to visit? Circle and say.**

1

2

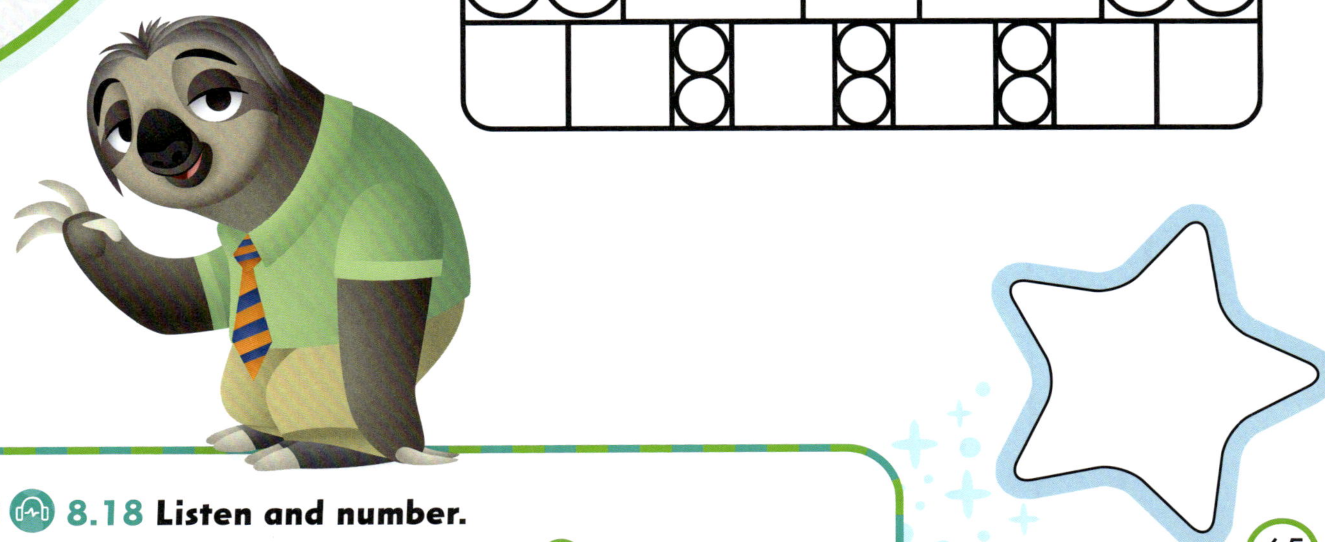

1 8.18 Listen and number.

2 Color the rectangles and triangles. What can you see? 3 Color your star.

9 My clothes

1

2

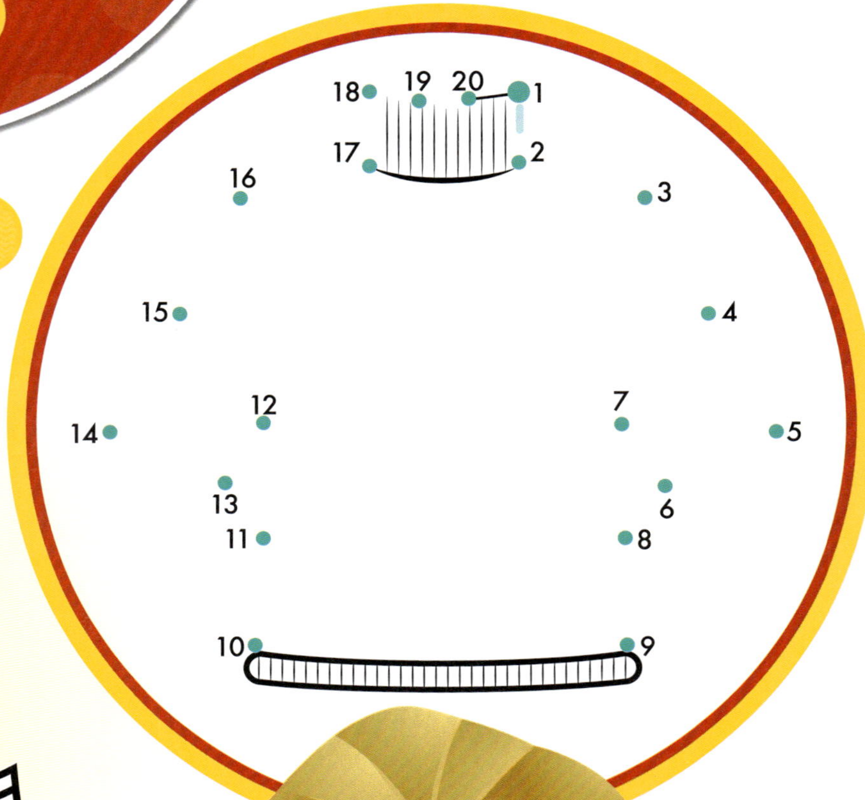

1 9.3 Listen and color. Say.

2 What's this? Join the dots and say.

1

2

1 9.7 **Listen, match, and say.**

2 **What are you wearing? Draw and say.**

I'm angry

1

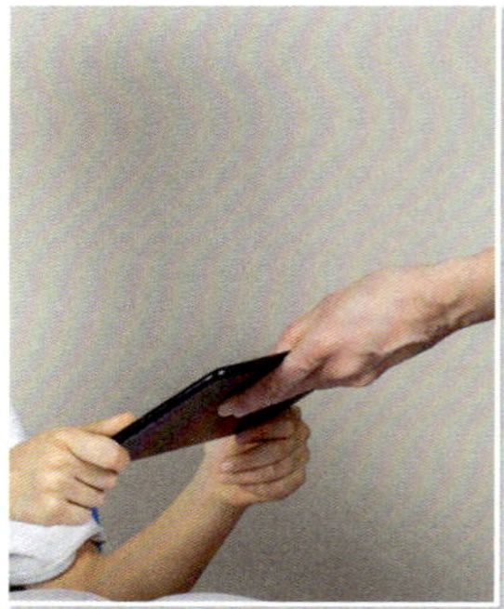

2

1 **Match and say.**

2 **What helps you when you're angry? Circle.**

1

11 12 13 14 15 16 17 18 19 20

2

1 9.12 Listen, find, and write numbers.

2 What's your favorite shape and color? Draw and color.

What does he want?

1 9.14 **Order the story (1–6). Then listen and check.**

2 **Color and say.**

I'm calm

1

2

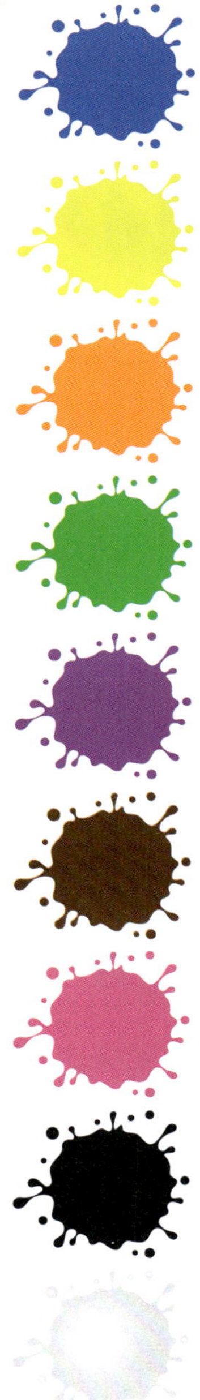

1 9.16 **Listen and trace.**

2 **Which color is calm for you? Check (✓) and say.**

My favorite clothes

1

2

1 9.18 **Listen and point. Then match and say.**

2 **Imagine you are at a party. Draw your costume.**

1

2

1 9.20 Listen and circle.

2 9.21 Listen, draw, and color. 3 Color your star.

Unit 1 | Unit 2

Aa

Aa

Ee

Ee

1 1.25 Listen and circle.
2 Join the dots, write, and say.

1 2.25 Listen and circle.
2 Join the dots, write, and say.

Unit 3 Unit 4

Ii

Ii

1 3.20 Listen and circle.
2 Join the dots, write, and say.

Oo

Oo

1 4.22 Listen and circle.
2 Join the dots, write, and say.

Unit 5 Unit 6

Uu

Uu

1 5.23 Listen and circle.
2 Join the dots, write, and say.

hat

hat

1 6.25 Listen and say.
2 Color and say. 3 Join the dots, write, and say.

Unit 7 | Unit 8

bed

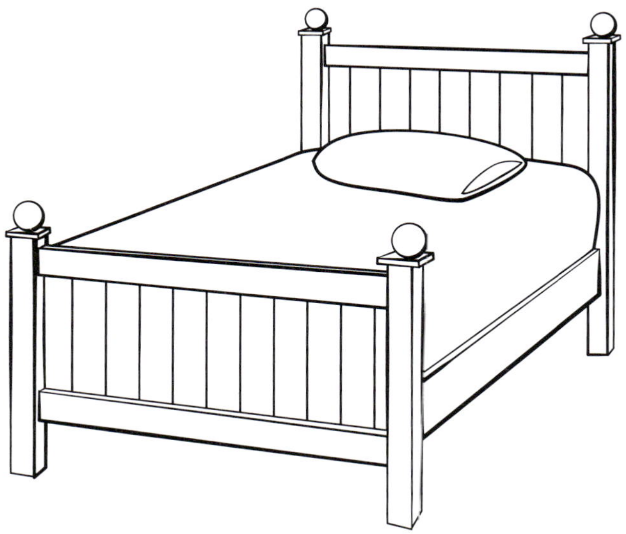

bed

1 7.20 Listen and say.
2 Color and say. 3 Join the dots, write, and say.

bus

bus

1 8.21 Listen and say. 2 Join the dots and say.
3 Join the dots, write, and say.

Unit 9

stop

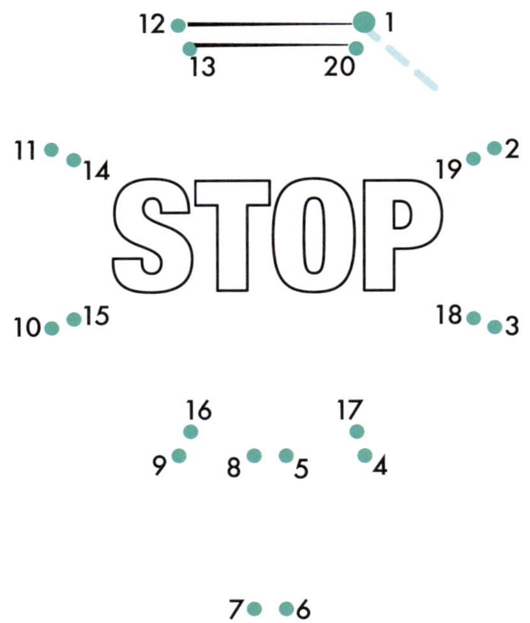

stop

1 9.24 Listen and say. 2 Join the dots and say.
3 Join the dots, write, and say.

1 My animals

2 My party

3 In the woods

4 In the sky

5 My senses

Aa Bb Cc Dd Ee Ff Gg Hh Ii Jj Kk Ll Mm

My learning path

Units 6–9

6 Let's go!

7 In the ocean

8 My city

9 My clothes

Nn Oo Pp Qq Rr Ss Tt Uu Vv Ww Xx Yy Zz